GRATITUDE JOURNAL

FOR

AWESOME KIDS

the ADVENTURES of
SCUBA JACK

Date __ / __ / __   SUN   MON   TUE   WED   THU   FRI   SAT

TODAY I AM THANKFUL FOR

- _____
- _____
- _____

SOMEONE WHO I THANKED TODAY

- _____
- _____

HAPINESS LEVEL

Draw or write about something you are good at

I AM THANKFUL FOR TODAY BECAUSE:

EMOTIONS I FELT TODAY

THIS IS WHAT MY DAY LOOKED LIKE

Draw or write about something that happened today

SOMEONE WHO I THANKED TODAY

Date __ / __ / __   Sun   Mon   Tue   Wed   Thu   Fri   Sat

TODAY I AM THANKFUL FOR

○ _____

○ _____

○ _____

SOMEONE WHO I THANKED TODAY

○ _____

○ _____

HAPINESS
LEVEL

Draw or write about something
you are good at

I AM THANKFUL FOR TODAY BECAUSE:

EMOTIONS I FELT TODAY

THIS IS WHAT MY DAY LOOKED LIKE

Draw or write about something that happened today

SOMEONE WHO I THANKED TODAY

Date __/__/__   Sun   Mon   Tue   Wed   Thu   Fri   Sat

TODAY I AM THANKFUL FOR

- _____
- _____
- _____

SOMEONE WHO I THANKED TODAY

- _____
- _____

HAPINESS
LEVEL

Draw or write about something
you are good at

I AM THANKFUL FOR TODAY BECAUSE:

EMOTIONS I FELT TODAY

THIS IS WHAT MY DAY LOOKED LIKE

Draw or write about something that happened today

SOMEONE WHO I THANKED TODAY

Date __ / __ / __   SUN   MON   TUE   WED   THU   FRI   SAT

TODAY I AM THANKFUL FOR

- _____
- _____
- _____

SOMEONE WHO I THANKED TODAY

- _____
- _____

HAPINESS
LEVEL

Draw or write about something
you are good at

I AM THANKFUL FOR TODAY BECAUSE:

EMOTIONS I FELT TODAY

THIS IS WHAT MY DAY LOOKED LIKE

Draw or write about something that happened today

SOMEONE WHO I THANKED TODAY

Date __ / __ / __   Sun   Mon   Tue   Wed   Thu   Fri   Sat

TODAY I AM THANKFUL FOR

- _____
- _____
- _____

SOMEONE WHO I THANKED TODAY

- _____
- _____

HAPINESS
LEVEL

Draw or write about something
you are good at

I AM THANKFUL FOR TODAY BECAUSE:

EMOTIONS I FELT TODAY

THIS IS WHAT MY DAY LOOKED LIKE

Draw or write about something that happened today

SOMEONE WHO I THANKED TODAY

TODAY I AM THANKFUL FOR

- _____
- _____
- _____

SOMEONE WHO I THANKED TODAY

- _____
- _____

HAPINESS
LEVEL

Draw or write about something
you are good at

I AM THANKFUL FOR TODAY BECAUSE:

EMOTIONS I FELT TODAY

THIS IS WHAT MY DAY LOOKED LIKE

Draw or write about something that happened today

SOMEONE WHO I THANKED TODAY

Date __ / __ / __   SUN   MON   TUE   WED   THU   FRI   SAT

TODAY I AM THANKFUL FOR

- _____
- _____
- _____

SOMEONE WHO I THANKED TODAY

- _____
- _____

HAPINESS
LEVEL

Draw or write about something
you are good at

I AM THANKFUL FOR TODAY BECAUSE:

EMOTIONS I FELT TODAY

THIS IS WHAT MY DAY LOOKED LIKE

Draw or write about something that happened today

SOMEONE WHO I THANKED TODAY

Date __ / __ / __   sun   mon   tue   wed   thu   fri   sat

TODAY I AM THANKFUL FOR

- ○ _____
- ○ _____
- ○ _____

SOMEONE WHO I THANKED TODAY

- ○ _____
- ○ _____

HAPINESS
LEVEL

Draw or write about something
you are good at

I AM THANKFUL FOR TODAY BECAUSE:

EMOTIONS I FELT TODAY

THIS IS WHAT MY DAY LOOKED LIKE

Draw or write about something that happened today

SOMEONE WHO I THANKED TODAY

Date __ / __ / __   SUN   MON   TUE   WED   THU   FRI   SAT

TODAY I AM THANKFUL FOR

- _____
- _____
- _____

SOMEONE WHO I THANKED TODAY

- _____
- _____

HAPINESS
LEVEL

Draw or write about something
you are good at

I AM THANKFUL FOR TODAY BECAUSE:

EMOTIONS I FELT TODAY

THIS IS WHAT MY DAY LOOKED LIKE

Draw or write about something that happened today

SOMEONE WHO I THANKED TODAY

Date __ / __ / __   SUN   MON   TUE   WED   THU   FRI   SAT

TODAY I AM THANKFUL FOR

- _____
- _____
- _____

SOMEONE WHO I THANKED TODAY

- _____
- _____

HAPINESS
LEVEL

Draw or write about something
you are good at

Date __/__/__   sun   mon   tue   wed   thu   fri   sat

I AM THANKFUL FOR TODAY BECAUSE:

EMOTIONS I FELT TODAY

THIS IS WHAT MY DAY LOOKED LIKE

Draw or write about something that happened today

SOMEONE WHO I THANKED TODAY

Date __ / __ / __   SUN   MON   TUE   WED   THU   FRI   SAT

TODAY I AM THANKFUL FOR

- _____
- _____
- _____

SOMEONE WHO I THANKED TODAY

- _____
- _____

HAPINESS
LEVEL

Draw or write about something
you are good at

Date __/__/__   Sun   Mon   Tue   Wed   Thu   Fri   Sat

I AM THANKFUL FOR TODAY BECAUSE:

EMOTIONS I FELT TODAY

THIS IS WHAT MY DAY LOOKED LIKE

Draw or write about something that happened today

SOMEONE WHO I THANKED TODAY

Date __ / __ / __   sun   mon   tue   wed   thu   fri   sat

TODAY I AM THANKFUL FOR

- _____
- _____
- _____

SOMEONE WHO I THANKED TODAY

- _____
- _____

HAPINESS
LEVEL

Draw or write about something
you are good at

I AM THANKFUL FOR TODAY BECAUSE:

EMOTIONS I FELT TODAY

THIS IS WHAT MY DAY LOOKED LIKE

Draw or write about something that happened today

SOMEONE WHO I THANKED TODAY

Date __ / __ / __   Sun   Mon   Tue   Wed   Thu   Fri   Sat

TODAY I AM THANKFUL FOR

- _____
- _____
- _____

SOMEONE WHO I THANKED TODAY

- _____
- _____

HAPINESS LEVEL

Draw or write about something
you are good at

I AM THANKFUL FOR TODAY BECAUSE:

EMOTIONS I FELT TODAY

THIS IS WHAT MY DAY LOOKED LIKE

Draw or write about something that happened today

SOMEONE WHO I THANKED TODAY

Date __ / __ / __   sun   mon   tue   wed   thu   fri   sat

TODAY I AM THANKFUL FOR

- _____
- _____
- _____

SOMEONE WHO I THANKED TODAY

- _____
- _____

HAPINESS
LEVEL

Draw or write about something
you are good at

Date __/__/__   SUN   MON   TUE   WED   THU   FRI   SAT

I AM THANKFUL FOR TODAY BECAUSE:

EMOTIONS I FELT TODAY

THIS IS WHAT MY DAY LOOKED LIKE

Draw or write about something that happened today

SOMEONE WHO I THANKED TODAY

Date __ / __ / __   sun   mon   tue   wed   thu   fri   sat

TODAY I AM THANKFUL FOR

- _____
- _____
- _____

SOMEONE WHO I THANKED TODAY

- _____
- _____

HAPINESS
LEVEL

Draw or write about something
you are good at

I AM THANKFUL FOR TODAY BECAUSE:

EMOTIONS I FELT TODAY

THIS IS WHAT MY DAY LOOKED LIKE

Draw or write about something that happened today

SOMEONE WHO I THANKED TODAY